The Music of the Aztecs

THE MUSIC OF THE AZTECS

EDITED AND WITH AN INTRODUCTION BY

David B Churchill

THE MUSIC OF THE AZTECS

Cover art: "Jane's Carousel" by Julienne Schaer
Book layout by Barbara Shaw

ISBN 978-0-9753095-4-4

First Edition

Published by:
Pony One Dog Press
PO Box 30552
Bethesda, Maryland 20824

Should we too have rules,
our clothes like
robes converse
instead of us—
Or unrobed meet
in honest pools
and freely speak our hearts?

CONTENTS

HOW TO USE THIS BOOK

THIS BOOK can change your life. This is a book of poetry and poems can do that. A poem can leave you in a state of heightened mindfulness. A poem can increase your understanding of yourself. A poem can further your personal growth. A good poem can contribute to spiritual development.

In this book a sampling of the work of the poets who belong to the Magic Theater Poetry Club have been collected in one place. The Magic Theater is among a plethora of venues, publishing opportunities and workshops dedicated to the craft of poetry in the Washington DC area. You can go to a coffee-house or restaurant somewhere any night of the week in this area and listen to poetry. There are journals, books and magazines, both printed and online, that publish quantities of new poetry by local, new and up-coming poets in the city and its environs. This book, a gathering of some of the best of it, is but a small reflection of this lively scene.

It is true, however, that you still find people here and there who do not read poetry. They may subscribe to the symphony, be in regular attendance at all the local theaters and avid readers to boot, but haven't picked up a book of poems since college.

This introduction is for them. It is for the person who says, "I came across those lines by William Carlos Williams the other day where he says, 'It is difficult to get the news from poems, yet men die miserably every day for lack of what is found there,' and not wanting to die miserably, I bought this book—now what? I don't know how to read poetry. I don't understand what it's about. —But I want to learn."

This is what I have to say: Poems exist in a Jungian matrix. Everything that's written down, including Holy Writ, is written by humans, and anything written by a human is subject to being influenced by all kinds of things, including, and perhaps especially, unconscious influences. And what a reservoir the unconscious is, where for millennia, when men lived in direct relation to Nature, it was coterminous with the world, taking the form of gods, angels, spirits, demons, souls of the departed and of course the ever-supplicated muse—now all corralled within each individual's psyche. Who knows now what its boundaries are, or what it holds, that once held all this? Indeed, who knows what its influences are?[1] They enter out of our unconscious, flow through us in our thoughts and feelings and out again through our words and actions. They bridge, from poet to reader and from person to person, the darkness within each of us that I believe connects us to our common humanity.

Perhaps the quickest way to use your new book then is for divination. It may be people don't use poetry for this purpose as often anymore, yet it's worth a look, and this practice has a long tradition. The ancients cut up poems like *The Aeneid*, for example, (*sortes virgilianae*) into strips of parchment, each containing one line. These strips were then used for sortilege, or divination by lots. More to be recommended, however—if you don't want to chop up a book you just paid $19.95 for—is the method employed by Saint Augustine. One day while walking in a garden, in a turmoil at his inability to heed the call to be baptized, he heard children playing next door. Suddenly one of their refrains came to him particularly clearly: "Take up and read! Take up and read!" Behind him on a table lay the book he had been reading, a collection of Christian writings. Picking it up, he opened it at random. The first words to strike his eye were: "Cease your chambering.... " (i. e. Latin for "stop whoring around"). The rest is history.

Using this book, if, for example, you wanted to know whether that hot guy or gal you just met on Tinder is interested in you, you might encounter these words on opening it at random:

> In short, whether Puritans or clowns
> Have picked a palette for the vacant clouds . . .

[1] Empirical psychology loved, until recently, to explain the "unconscious" as mere absence of consciousness—the term itself indicates as much—just as shadow is an absence of light. Today accurate observation of unconscious processes has recognized, with all other ages before us, that the unconscious possesses a creative autonomy such as a mere shadow could never be endowed with. Carl Jung; CW 11: *Psychology and Religion: West and East*; Page 14.

a beautiful image from a poem by Reid Baron, and conclude that they were; or these evocative words from a poem by Marianne Szlyk:

> The birds' notes replace the rain
> during this dry summer.

and decided they weren't: both verses describe emptiness and loss, what you might feel at the possibility that this person isn't interested, or the feelings that may have motivated you to look for someone on a dating app in the first place.

One strategy to make it easier to understand a poem is the presence of an argument in a poem. Because of the way the mind works, if a poet has something to say, the statement usually falls into a well-known structure. The pattern consists of a premise (or question), a complication (or two or three) and a final resolution (or further question). This format is more commonly seen in traditional poetry, such as the work of Donne and Shakespeare. Typically philosophical, sentimental or sympathetic in nature, the argumentative form tended to be given up in the modern period as being too predictable—but still can be found in even the simplest poems of some of the most modern of modern poets. Consider "The Red Wheelbarrow" by William Carolos Williams:

> so much depends
> upon
>
> a red wheel
> barrow
>
> glazed with rain
> water
>
> beside the white
> chickens.

Here the premise is "so much depends upon"; the complication "a red wheel barrow," and the resolution is "glazed with rain." This schema can be paraphrased as "life is contingent (depends on), human effort (red wheel barrow) is inadequate to address that contingency, unless aided by the transcendent (glazed with rain)." Read this way, the poem's meaning comes clear as a comment on the writing of poetry itself, which though it "depends" on human effort, must be furthered by inspiration. Indeed, it is conceivable that life is such that no human effort alone is enough unless aided by something beyond our control, described here in terms of Nature-images, an image of fecundity and a highly original (and homely) image of chickens, (standing affectively in for more traditional bird-of-flight symbolism). As compact as the poem is, it still falls into a very comprehensible dialectic.

Not every poem can be wrapped up so neatly. Applying the argument pattern to Marianne Szlyk's "The Social Work Assistant in Briarwood," in this collection, we find ourselves taken by surprise as Marianne uses the form's predictability to lead us in a totally unexpected direction. The first stanza states the premise:

> In another life,
> you lived here, place
> that time and the city
> forgot. You
> would become mute here.

The speaker is talking to a friend, describing her existence, one where she feels stifled. We continue to be led along as details take visual form through the next three stanzas that elaborate on her situation, where "words clogged your throat" like "mustard greens, blue / cornbread, his truth," where life was stuck in the past, the sun squeezed "through tiny panes" and all she could do was write ineffectual notes. The last stanza delivers its surprise. Where we expected a resolution of some kind, the poem turns back to its beginning—now with an added layer of despair: "Leaves and thorns / grew over glass." The misery is deepened as it is completed.

Contrast this poem with the first poem in the collection by Jan Claire Starkey, "At the Swimming Pool." The same pattern can be discerned here as well, though again, its resolution is not as we expect.

After a brief stanza that sets the scene, the premise is stated as the speaker confesses how easy it would be to drown, just "letting the water fill my lungs like humid air."

Two stanzas follow, each stating a complication, here nicely played off against each other. The lifeguards are described as playing a prank, rather than remaining vigilant for such children as the speaker described herself to be in the premise, who might act on their temptation, and in the following stanza, where the speaker feels "clean and satisfied"—strangely undismayed by the lifeguards' indifference.

Now we are awake to surprises, and the resolution does not disappoint:

> Whenever it got dark, Mary Ann and I
> pretended to be mermaids,
> together and separate in the hazy underwater silence—
> The pool lights turning into moons.

and we are left to explore a comforting, dream-like world of mermaids and moons with a friend, as we wonder at this strange turn of events, not at all confused or left behind as we followed.

Divination and the argument pattern aside, another way readers get the most out of poetry is by bringing something to it, their experiences and imaginations in addition to their needs and questions. The interpretation of poems is not unlike the interpretation of dreams. T.S. Eliot once said poetry communicates its meaning before it's fully understood, and this is especially true when we encounter poetry with a forward-looking mind, projecting out of our lives, through the poem, into the future. As with anything else of this nature, a dream, a deck of Tarot cards, poetry requires interpretation. Even Jesus spoke in parables, lest the uninitiated "comprehend and be saved."

We each have within us our own keys to interpretation, and one of the values of poetry—perhaps its greatest—is that by its mere existence we are forced to look to our keys, whether or not we ever apply them. A key to interpretation is like a gate to the unconscious; it is for the lack of this that men and women die—if not miserably—at least uncomprehendingly, like animals. To be awake to our full potential as humans requires us to be wholly integrated. Poems, like Tarot cards, have the power to bring us to that integration, if we allow it.

To find the key to a poem's meaning within yourself, it may be helpful to start with something simple, something that is of interest to you. I have always been intrigued, for example, by parental figures in poetry and how poets write about them. For the purpose of illustration then, let's look at a couple.

In Reid Baron's "Between Me, The Sea and My Old Man,, the speaker is saying goodbye to his elderly father in a place by the sea. The father is a veteran and the shore here, through its opposites of land and water, suggests not just the taking leave of one's earthly form but other moments of decision, personal, historical and existential, that both men have faced or are facing now. At first it is the gulf between generations that stands in relief:

> The clouds stack up
> Much the same as they do
> over Cosumel or Negril
> When I asked him if this
> Resembled Pago Pago
> He said the Japs there
> Fell right out of the trees

Traditionally a figure of authority, in the unconscious the father-image becomes a nexus for issues of self-confidence and authenticity. Thus in this seemingly innocent moment, in the father's misunderstanding response to his son's question, his answering out of his own past rather than to the present and the son who is before him, we feel the impossibility of a connection, the failure of the world of the Greatest Generation to pass its certainties and assertions on to its own successors. As the speaker states wryly, "Dad... / Made me / Step out into this predicament."

In the few last lines, mirroring the dwindling of the father's consciousness, we come to a gentle and heart-warming resolution:

> Just about everyone bent
> Said his piece:

Easy does it.
Thanks

Very different from this is a picture—not of a father—but of a father figure, the Peruvian poet Cesar Vallejo. In a poem of the same name, Alan Britt lets the images speak for themselves.

Volcanic eyes

Aardvark gait

Soul a chrysalis & also
a papoose to tuck his family
into at night

Dreams swirled like
Van Gogh's Starry Night

His poems were fists
full of scorpions

The speaker is obviously describing a man of anger and violence. You can almost see him punching his wife, his children. But within this outline, the portrait becomes more nuanced. Here was a man who was ungainly in life, hobbled perhaps by what might have been considered at the time an "unmanly" softness for his family, a man who was moreover a dreamer. Now we see more clearly the speaker's father-figure was a man on the defensive, a man not beating up on his wife and children, but in conflict with a world that didn't accept him for what he was, a man with an emotional, more "feminine" temperament.

The biggest problem in reading poetry, however, afflicting lay readers and lovers of poetry alike, is the speed at which we normally read nowadays. As a society, we're so used to gulping down quantities of prose, and so strapped for time, that slender verses on a page seem to dart through our eyes like trout. No wonder we come away empty and frustrated, convinced the fault must be in us, hungrier than before for what poetry has to give us.

Take a look at "Taxonomy of History," by Ethan Goffman. Ethan's poems generally read well at a "normal" speed and this poem is no exception, but at the end the last lines flash by so quickly you're hardly aware you've seen them, let alone what they said:

> Still they are thunderstorms, pummeling fields of cantankerous,
> yearning weeds,
> young weeds that spout from drenched soil and spew outlaw seeds.

Nevertheless, *something* sticks in your mind, for you immediately pause and re-read them. They are likely the most interesting lines in the whole poem.

Many of today's poems arrive in short, concentrated lines, chock-a-block with metaphors and other literary allusions. Most of us probably don't even have the patience any more for the long leisurely prosody of the past. (See if you still don't need to slow yourself down at places in the early poems of Yeats, for example.) So I'm afraid there's no help for the problem but to approach it seriously.

Read a poem first at normal speed. If there's anything in it for you, you'll feel it. (Remember: a poem doesn't always have to be fully understood to communicate its meaning.) Book-mark the page. When you're ready to go back to it, turn to that page again with this question in mind: what does this have to say to me? Now that you're looking for something, you'll find it more easy to read slowly.

Speak each line out loud. Explain to yourself, preferably out loud too, what each line means as you read it. Take it word by word. You may only need to do this a few times before you find yourself automatically slowing each time you begin reading. Merely slowing down opens your sense to the possibility of reading more closely. This is when poetry begins to get interesting.

Read the following highly-evocative poem from John MacDonald at the same speed you are reading this. See if you don't get a feeling from it before you know what it's about.

Only

small gods in grass floor chapels,
floating through open roof,
open air, smoking

in small volcanoes,
exchanging sacrifice
for accident, waiting

in wrinkled bark
of ancient trees like
totem grandparents,

we are only warm
sweetmetal earth,
sun and stars and
nothing more.

You *will* wait
and watch us,
nothing more.

Already you get a sense of an invisible kingdom, paralleling our world, like the world of spirits I started this introduction with. That these small gods inhabit nature seems obvious. The Romans built shrines to them in the forest and held certain groves to be sacred to them, as the line "totem grandparents" seems to suggest. The words "exchanging sacrifice / for accident" also seems to suggest what happens when we stop honoring them. In the fourth stanza the gods address us directly, and in view of what has gone before about "sacrifice" and "waiting / in wrinkled bark", the lines at the end, "You will wait / and watch us" takes on the force of a command (italics mine).

There is much more here, and certainly mine is not the only interpretation. But this is a good poem to practice with, especially as it reinforces the way our workaday world is interpenetrated by the universe of numinosities and influences with which I began this essay.

In the words of the children, "Take up and read!" Keep in mind the techniques for understanding poetry as you browse through this book, then go back and read it again. Ours is a world on a tightrope, strung between other worlds. Poems are written on the veil between worlds, and where they are, the veil is a little thinner.

Rumors of Stars

MARIANNE SZLYK

If My Mother is in Purgatory

she is a stewardess, flying
through turbulence, never crashing, never
landing. Her skirt is too
short, showing each half-pound
creeping onto her small frame.
She cannot stop to pull
down her skirt or reapply
her makeup or fix her
hair or even drink coffee.

The passengers plead for more
for more drinks for more
pillows more peanuts more sickbags.
Customers call for more quiet
as babies and grown men
howl as fat women pray
to Jesus without a rosary.
She rolls her eyes, correcting
everyone's grammar in her mind.

Her coworkers are friends. They
roll their eyes as, voices
lowered, they discuss the passengers.
While they stock the cart,
they give everyone nicknames. They
have nicknames for coworkers, too.
They can't find pillows; they
fill the cart with blankets
or raincoats or sticky uniforms.

They can't find Dramamine; they
raid their purses for M&Ms
breath mints or hard candy.

Someday this plane will land.
My mother swears that she
will go back to Maine
and never leave. Her friends
and family will all have
to find her there.

The Social Work Assistant in Briarwood

In another life,
you lived here, place
that time and the city
forgot. You
would become mute here.

Too thick to speak,
words clogged your throat. You could
breathe. You swal-
lowed mustard greens, blue
cornbread, his truth.

You drank coffee. You just
did not talk.
Radio stuck on
the Sixties, sun squee-
zing through tiny panes,

you wrote notes.
You drank Diet Pepsi.
You ate slices of
pudding cake. Your husband
talked. Your friends

did, too. Leaves and thorns
grew over glass.
The sun turned back. Only
memories
of its touch remained.

Astoria at Dawn

Nobody braves the city street,
black as an iced-over river
between cars like snow banks.

Behind blinds a man lingers
over coffee, its taste bitter
enough to slice through sleep's
thick fog. He pours in
cream and sugar. Sleep sneaks
back, washing through him. Sweet
coffee cannot buoy him up.

His wife lies awake beneath
blankets as white as dreams
of summer's clouds.

Saturday Morning

R Street NW, Washington DC

Girls with yoga mats walk in the rain
through a dream of green
beside sycamore trees,
beneath linden trees.

They talk through the rain,
their hair as smooth as shadows,
their flip-flops slapping
through puddles.

The rain falls like pin-pricks
on their bare arms,
against their tank tops.
Mimosa blossoms
stick in their hair.

Soon they will be
inside.
They will salute the sun
that will not show
its face today.

Abandoned

June bamboo swallows
the bite-sized house. Sharp, green teeth
pierce darkness within.

Rooftop antenna
pulls in static. Red-winged black-
birds perch on its arms.

Humidity blooms
inside and out. Summer rain
curls up in the tub.

Paper coffee cups
clatter on bare floors. Dust
specks rise, caught in webs.

Empty hangers chat-
ter in the bedroom closet.
Bats greet another dusk.

The Summer After the Bridge Closed

In the absence of lawn mowers, the sparrow's
song flows down slate tiles,
over brick walls and wooden window sills
to the rocks at island's edge.

Fat black crows strut down
the streets where grass will grow.
Without hawks or humans,
birds have no need to fly.

Waves crash onto smaller stones
that gather next to the rocks.
The ocean's fingers crumble
the beach as if it were a cracker.

For now, starlings emerge
from rhododendron and boxwood.
The birds' notes replace the rain
during this dry summer.

Yet the grass is greener. Clover
mingles with chicory and milkweed.
Long grass sways in the wind.
It flowers.

The Last Days of Fusion

As saxophone and piano washed
past doorways, the couple walked
down the street, looking to
enter places they would have
never dared three years ago.

December snow fell in spurts.
She clenched, then unclenched gray
gloved hands in the pocket
of her teal wool coat.
His coat was new, too.

Already places were shutting down.
This was not New York,
not Manhattan. His friend Elgar
had died. So they couldn't
visit him in his three-decker,
so close to Harvard Square.

In the last days of fusion,
the couple walked on Mass Ave.,
avoiding their memories of Elgar,
nights they'd spent drinking tonic
and listening to Miles Davis
on crackling vinyl, to Elgar
cracking his jokes, telling his stories
about Cambridge in the Thirties.

Fine snow became light rain,
summoning the smell of damp wool.

A guitarist exited the cafe,
looking for his car as
the last trackless trolley fled
down Trapelo Road. In doorways,
the young men played horns,
making the old songs fizz
like soda with lime.

Facing East at Dawn

After a photograph by Northscapes Photography, Presque Isle, ME

The driftwood is a hand grasping something
then letting it go. Stars scatter above
as if this hand

had tossed them into the morning sky.
Up there, they grow brighter. They will
fade once sunrise washes away night.

Yet there is light now. Stars band
together into the Milky Way. Clouds form
like clusters of maple leaves clinging to water.

The water is itself. It reflects nothing.
It rests beneath the sky, awaiting sunrise
and its long day as a sparkling mirror.

It contains everything: cans, rocks, hornpout, weeds.
Before dawn its splash on the shore
is quieter. No birds break its surface.

Across the lake, someone's car rounds the curve
from the next town nearer to sunrise.
Its light is a fallen star. Soon others will follow.

Alternative History in Staunton, Virginia

The man who sings my favorite song
wanders the streets of this small city.
He no longer carries his guitar,
too heavy for walking past seventy
on uneven brick sidewalks
that all run uphill.

An ex-smoker,
he catches his breath
beneath the marquee
of the last one-screen movie theater,
the one that used to show
movies he liked.
It reeks of buttered popcorn.
He moves on

past the site
of the old Woolworth's,
the one that sold his records
back when they were hits,
when they floated out of windows
even in this mountain town,

before they clung to him,
never leaving the room
with the reel to reel tape,
never leaving home.

Riding into Charles Street Station

The river wasn't yet someone else's necklace.
I glimpsed it on my way to work,
looking up from a book my boss had given me
about someone else's city, one
I planned to return to someday.

Crew teams were scuttling home down the silver river
to breakfast and their first class, the mathematics
that would have freed me from typewriter
and telephone, from this two-hour commute
that ended at the ocean, the physics
that would have kept me from
my residents and coworkers at Long Island Hospital.

I imagined walking alongside the river,
even just crossing it on foot
in sunlight that glittered on the water
like glass, like borrowed costume jewelry
and in the sunset that would stain it orange.

I imagined living near the river,
perhaps in the building I saw
right before entering the tunnel.
I would grow used to the sight of
trains before midnight and the black waters
after. The river would stay in my mind
the way that my aunt's gift of pearls did,
kept for special occasions, therefore
never worn.

But the river was always someone else's necklace.
A dumpy girl in nylons and pastels, not
dressed for success, not even wearing earrings,
I was passing through on a subway car
that was often filled with others
blocking my view of the river.
Most of them had a better right
to this necklace than I did.

I was biding my time, waiting
to leave for some other city,
some other river that I could
touch and taste and smell,
a river that was not of jewelry.

Rainy Living

"You participate in the raining; your existence is a rainy living."
Paul F. Schmidt, "Kyoto Temples"

On the other side of the window,
rain falls. Cypress drips.
Glancing out, I sip ginger tea.

I'm not here. I'm in the Northwest
of moss and fern, tree trunks
green not brown, houses

tucked in beneath spruce
and cedar, mountains today
hidden in fog, in trees.

I'm not here. There's no school.
Flakes fall from a deadpan sky
covering over grass,

forgotten coffee cups,
water bowls for long-dead cats.
I sit and read prose

about the rain in Kyoto.
It seems gentle, steady,
falling without wind pushing

through rice paper walls
or sweeping cold water inside.
Here the rain pours

onto the skylight above me,
slaps the sides of the yellow house,
blots out the sound of traffic.

I participate in the raining.

Woolworth's, 1970

She remembers the lunch counter
in her grandmother's city,
half a day's drive on backroads
to smaller towns in Canada.

She didn't remember anyone black
at the counter or in the stores.
She remembers ordering a hamburger
like Grandma did, never looking
at the cracked, greasy menu.

She remembers cages
of green parakeets,
the thick smell of popcorn,
heaps of butts and ash
in the ashtrays on the counter.
"The Long and Winding Road"
billowed out from the record shop
speakers like curtains in the summer.

She wonders how different
this Woolworth's was
from the one in Greensboro,
in 1960.
She thinks to ask her grandmother

but knows she never will

York Beach, 2006

On a summer night without even
a ceiling fan to stir sludgy air,
I open the window to ocean,
the susurrus of waves and cars.
People almost my age weave home.
They've been drinking at Long Sands,
watching the moonlight shatter high tide.
Lying on the couch to escape
the stifling guest room, I dream
I'm back in my grandmother's house
where, at 107, Gram's still alive,
a tall woman shrunken
to an abandoned rag doll
on a beige mohair armchair.

Clutching the railing, fearing the stairs
will not bear weight, I climb
to where now only spiders live.
I open windows to flashing sirens,
fire trucks racing down Lunenburg Street
over the bluster of men walking
home with cans of malt liquor
from Minit Mart where Gram bought
hamburger and pink tomatoes.
I spring awake to the quiet
of an oceanfront house.
My elderly parents sleep below.
I lie back down, wondering what

my grandmother would have told me,
what I would have done next
in this other world.

A Sibyl of Fortune

JAN CLAIRE STARKEY

At the Swimming Pool

Summer days spent at the pool that I rode my bike to,
past the green hills
of a newly made golf course.

When I learned how to hold my breath
and swim two lengths,
I almost passed out when my head
started pounding. Then I knew
how easy it would be to drown,
just falling asleep,
letting the water fill my lungs like humid air.

Once, the lifeguards staged a nighttime
pool party
and put scores of goldfish into the water …

That feeling of taking a shower,
exhausted and clean and satisfied.
A lingering smell of chlorine
and strawberry-scented shampoo.

Whenever it got dark, Mary Ann and I
pretended to be mermaids,
together and separate in the hazy underwater silence—
The pool lights turning into moons.

Duality

She is mean and crippled in her bad mood.
She is clean and wicked in her small room.
She is white and wretched in her dull mind.
She is gold and stupid in her green home.
She is ripe and pretty in her mild luck.
She is earth and water in her full moon.
She is glue and saintly in her nice brain.
She is ground in fury like her strong poem.
You art dust and empty in her dead womb.

To Sleep

Drowsy dying tones, kettle-drum, slumberous ...
Noiseless as pain, my breath filling the room.
My hair, like sea-weed, bunches of knot-grass, flowers ...
I sleep with wakeful visions, syllables and roses –
keeping my eyelids closed, blissfully until tomorrows …

Above the Labyrinth

O Icarus
the sun is rising
against a paper white sky
your wings beating with brilliance

wave upon wave upon wave
he came to light

Consider Icarus—
against that spectacle of sky,
the sun turned
red.
And you who watch notice nothing—
notice nothing.
What a glorious sight!

In dreams, you see the sun
half swallowed by water

Before he learned how to die, Icarus
turned around
to see his father's face
trusting his instincts
to fly.

That day
the moon outlived the sun.
Starlight cast
shadows on Icarus.

Stars, stars on the night sky
and your son, dead to the moon—
Under whose oceantide,
Icarus?

They say the sun fell
while he rose from his seagrave.

And when the water covered his body,
I couldn't cry or watch—it was too much.
So I sat at the edge of the pier.
Shut-out, afraid, numb,
I waited for something or someone
to catch my eye.

In the blue hour of morning,
the sea mirrors the moon.
Though I see stars so finely
attuned to the night, a wave, a light—

Once surrounded,
he couldn't be seen after all.
I couldn't see him after all.

God

a cup of blood
wine, with bread
and the good
sense (not)
to spill it.

Art Story

They found his wings, unattached,
floating to the shoreline.
Shells collected in the feathers,
some still burying into the soft wax.

On the sand, his wings lay glittering –
the sun directly over – stopped,
like a picture.

So he was only a man after all.

Missouri Was a State of Mind

Taking cold showers at church camp and sleeping
on those teeny green bugs that
clung to our pillows.

She turned the air conditioner up so high
it blew my bangs away. Her blue Horizon.

We discovered hair curlers on our way to voluptuous.
I had to buy her romances because she was too embarrassed.

Terricloth short-sets stuck to sweat.
And all those greasy fish filets we bought.

Backyard football and piling in mud.
Long talks of virginity and its real worth—we
never decided that one. Harlequins were enough.

(I hated that slush.) Sliding down snow
in huge black inner tubes. (I just did it for her.)

Fake belly-dancing—"Only the Good Die Young"
until her mother forbade such sacrilege—
she broke the record. So we bought a new one
and played it softly.

I think it might have been sex or
that Boonesfarm Strawberry Hill she praised;
but when she left for her Sterling Heights
in Chrysler county Michigan,
I bottled my Missouri—
and placed it high on my bedroom shelf.

The Sphinx

by Rodin

I am climbing out of white rock
curious to see whose
face will meet mine—

in another life.
I am half god, half animal.
I scare you with my pure stare.

There, My Love

The steps are uneven, wobbly,
familiar yet never familiar.
We walk as if we will never touch ground.

It is dark and the street lamps are flames.
So long with the one who knows me, my love.
A single star above the Rome-like buildings —
Mirrors and sky.
The houses go on forever
with their ice cream windows.
Over here, the road leads away
but we don't have to go there.

Kingdom without Space

"Time is a child . . . " –Carl Jung

I see the veins of leaves,
the green reign of restful sleep . . .
Come to the window!
Come away with us!

My breath fogs up the glass,
my eyes cast over the valleys
where there are thousands of suns¬—
the kingdom without space,
the future, erased
while it happens.

I walk on water then sink in silky sand
to touch like moss
the feathery goo
of wombs and caves.
I fly like swimming:
there is no difference
between air and liquid.

Sir, your magic tricks don't fool me.
I am too lithe and clever
for your immortality.
Instead, I run away
and you can't catch me.

I will resolve your dreams
without mercy

and you will feel
as if you died—

Aboard the boat Charon drives
we are the ghosts
along for the ride.

Eurydice's Excuse

–The wound is the muse.

You went to hell because you wanted me back.
The mirror cracked and our luck ran out.

I sat in a bar with flame-colored walls
where demons wailed their off-key songs
a language garbled in twangs and coughs
and chunks of vomit stuck in the throat.

I wandered there when you disappeared—
Snake-ridden, I
sickened and began to die.

When you walked into the smoke to catch my eye.
and waited by me through the morning dark
while I drank my fill of absinthe.

I went to hell because I wanted you back.
I turned back the clock and forgot . . .

Magic Castles

And the blue lights like glowing
butterflies keep me company—
They call to my blue soul.

I remember the little girl I was
by the creek when the snow
and I made canopies, magic castles—

I got lost in time in a winter forest.
Photos of windows, bright blue
shutters, cattails in the garden.

I make a circle of little loops,
winding motions of thoughts
to hang myself on.

A Lost Time

"Time is the moving image of eternity." –Plato

The sea by the beach house
that my grandmother kept
over decades of summers.
She wore diamonds
that sparkled like the moon
over the purple water.

And the carnival lights
at the turn of evenings, bright
with death the electric thrum.
Where pictures in the albums come from—
my childhood, hobby horses and tilt-a-whirls,
clown faces and pink candy.

Blue pincers of crabs
that fishermen cut off,
scattered on the boardwalk.
Tiny clams, like opalescent
flecks of paint, scurried
under the sand as waves
pulled back into themselves.

I watched the stars cover the sky
that held the water,
the moving images of black and white.

Across the Sea

Gigantic houses lined the sand—
facades swimming pool blue,
like Van Gogh's *Church at Auvers*,
and the stars outside the attic
window I climbed up to
where the waves crash in my memory
less distant than the present,
and my cousins asleep while the sound of water
rolling into and over itself,
like heavy breathing, and
the ancients whispered from their lost worlds.

I wandered alone into nightshadows
under the moon's orange clouds
waiting for faeries to enter my dreams,
to take me flying
across the sea towards the tesseract
where Meg and Calvin and Charles adventured—
beautiful beyond music.

JAN CLAIRE STARKEY

Before I was Scared of the Dark

For Caddy

you go on into the house go on now I am dont cry Im bad
anyway you cant help it theres a curse on us its not our fault
is it our fault hush come on and go to bed now

–William Faulkner

Sun-drunk ladies toasted caramel-brown,
stretched out on green and white striped plastic
lounge chairs, baking in bikinis,
chain smoking cigarettes,
sipping gin from orange and gold tumblers

by the swimming pool where Jimmy McClellan taught us
how to whirl around in the shallow end,
his blue eyes flickering with the water,
his cherry-flavored red smile.

Dense woods led there—
the road running by my house just ended in forest,
where someone spotted a racer-head after a heavy rainfall.

Purple stickyweeds grew like wishing flowers,
their summer scent intense.
Georgia heat, film-coated puddles,
mosquitoes, heavy with pregnancy.
We sweated and cooled down with the garden hose.

Houses half-built on cinderblocks,
boards and nails stuck in the clay.

Inside, we played "Dark Shadows,"
like hide and seek, waiting for a vampire kiss.

The first time I tried to leave home, I was seven.
I climbed out of my second story window,
grabbed hold the limbs of the birch tree
and shimmied down the drainpipe.

In my bare-feet, I stirred the grasses of cut lawns
while the night whistles of a distant train
pulsed like music in my earblood,
calling me away from there for good.

Small Gods

JOHN MACDONALD

Smooth Glass Child

you reach with transparent hand
for a balloon
curving light around you

arms outstretched you spin
like fine silk
near the window

but it's not enough to press
your hand
against the pane

you must draw a flower
into dew
clinging the edge

because you are a
smooth
glass child

Elder Emeritus

here am
I busted old
bro/ken
like a broken
old crucifix how
would you
feel after
jesus hung
on you that
many years?

JOHN MACDONALD

More Oceans

I wish there were more oceans
holding glorious blue cold
waters swelling with islands,
you know,

and other
breathing things
to grow atop them.

That's the thing I want,
those things that grow on top.

I would look in their eyes and imagine
their counterpoints in the deep
oceans I wish existed.

Only

small gods in grass floor chapels,
floating through open roof,
open air, smoking

in small volcanoes,
exchanging sacrifice
for accident, waiting

in wrinkled bark
of ancient trees like
totem grandparents,

we are only warm
sweetmetal earth,
sun and stars and
nothing more.

You will wait
and watch us,
nothing more.

JOHN MACDONALD

I Hope You're Dreaming of New Mexico

I hope
you're dreaming
          of
New Mexico
like

a Kokopelli
sleepwalker
          who bumps
into a wooden
chair one night
in his
adobe hut.

If it were daybreak
he would see
the chair
was painted a
          simple
light
blue

quiet

waiting for
the sun to
          set fire
to the mountains.

Imaginary Sun

Make me a diamond
from pure twilight
built on early planets
shining

as we,
in darkness,

content ourselves
with imaginary
sun.

Blanket Weavers

I dreamed we were blanket weavers
covering the children,

covering young lovers making
secret promises,

covering old men and old women
making good on those promises,

and at day's end
we would

become children, lovers
and old men and women

under a blanket
of stars.

The Music of the Aztecs

ETHAN GOFFMAN

Laughter Makes the World Go Round

I can't spread love
because I just don't have enough.
But I'd love to spread laughter,
carry it like cash
spilling from my pockets

hand it out to strangers, friends, colleagues,
even enemies
as tips
as advice
as succulent nibbles.

Laughter is double edged
Anger is its father
a blade that slices
leaving raw wounds in tender flesh

Anger is those wounds
and salt in those wounds
and venom in that salt.

So I won't spread anger
and I can't spread love
I'm no cupid with a quiver full of arrows
My love quiver is straight out empty.

What arrows I do have are more ambiguous
with spikes and sharp edges
I'd love to shoot them about randomly
aiming straight and true.

Laughter in my quiver
laughter in my pocket
an ointment rich and creamy
cool and invigorating.
A salve that transmutes
water into wine
pigshit into gold.

When My Wife Gave Birth

When my wife gave birth,
she gave birth to cats.
A feisty calico
and a tabby
who purred so loud
it about shook the world.

I said Isn't something the matter?
Don't most women
give birth to human babies
and not cats?

She threw me a look
half glance, half glare
as if to say
What more did you expect,
you who could never give birth to anything?

In all likelihood
my wife and I will survive our children
leaving us lonely and alone
to live out our days.

The Force Is Not With Me

I am the guy in a red shirt in every episode of Star Trek
Who dies in the first scene or two.
I am not Spock.
I am not Kirk.
I am not the guest vixen in a low-cut blouse and mini-skirt.
I am Crew Member #3.

In our own minds we are all the hero
A colossus astride history,
Xena, Warrior Princess.

A wise man
who realized his true significance in the Great Script of Life
recently threw himself in front of the morning metro train.

I was late for work.
How thoughtless of him.

Music of the Aztecs

Hearts ripped from bodies, rivers of blood
Punctuated by the frenzied heartbeat of drums
soothed by the soul of woodwinds

We will never hear Aztec music

A barbaric civilization
Wiped out in rivers of blood
By Conquistadors
bearing Christian civilization

Books burned, legends silenced

There must have been many beautiful days,
in the womb of Aztec civilization
lovers admiring sunrise
flutes snaking melodies
sun glinting off pyramids
a courtier asleep in the noon heat

The music remains
in imagination
misty lies

Some myths were not lost
Tezcatlipoca and Quetzalcoatl
smoked mirror and feathered serpent,
their names a convoluted music

The two smiled upon humanity, conspired,
to steal music from the temple of the sun,
bring it to Earth, to the Aztec people
to fill their days with life

Later they fought,
two gods going at each other like jaguars in heat,
Tezcatlipoca tormenting Quetzalcoatl
like a conquistador torturing the last Aztec

my poor imagination can't begin to conjure up the ghosts
of melody and jagged rhythm
lost until the sun grows cold

YouTube can serve up a facsimile in an instant
but no technology can conjure up
a deeper magic
nor can poetry's humble words

We can only recreate
a kind of cartoon of the Aztecs
the marvel comics version

Blood and sacrifice
war and worship
drums vibrating
a ghostly facsimile

Taxonomy of History

There are three main branches in the study of History:

The History of the Past
The History of What Happened
The History of What the Hell Happened!

The last, less respected than the others, is sometimes known as
The History of One Damned Thing After Another.

There are three even less reputable branches of history:

The History of the Future
The History of What Might Have Happened
The History of What Never Happened

Most historians don't recognize these branches. Even some of
the more refined poets look down upon them.

Still they are thunderstorms, pummeling fields of cantankerous,
yearning weeds,
young weeds that spout from drenched soil and spew outlaw
seeds

Night Ark

ANNIE FINCH

Spells

From music, I bore
Some gold-stone fins,
but they sank away
through the waffled shallows.

From nature, I gleaned
Some hope of rice—
But it edged deep away
In sunk stone bowls.

So then I asked
For bowls and fins;
I asked for a hand
that couild gather them back

into finning the shallows,
gilding, rounding.
I guessed me a hand
That could gather bowls open.

When I had asked
Whom I had guessed,
She sent my asking out.

Now over and over
she sends it back.
Over and over it answers me.

Over and over it answers, as she gives it,
in the speech of fins, and in the speech of bowls.

Drunken Iconographers

REID BARON

Tapachulteca

Merida 3/6/73

Already a legend she entered town
With Santa Barbara of the green ribbons.
In the midnight they made a comely pair
And filled the plaza with men-in-waiting.
(We kept our distance and stayed up late,
thinking.)

Morning came, and a day to fill with
Mayan majesty in ruins. Playing hunches,
We boarded the second bus, and setting out
Passed the birds in parti-colored plumage,
Shoeless and be-ribboned.
You wanted to get down!
Who cared for time and timeless architecture,
Just one word, my darling…

Dumbfounded by the mushroom, surrounded
By Connecticut elderly tiring too, of airplanes
And pyramids; into the debate of this and that—
Those flawless French who twittered beaux cheval sauvage
Because he kicked his heels—
The guides, the frauds, the couples
Blurred through corners of elixir vision.

Strode (in plumage) la de Tapa.
And her escort Santa Barbara
Glorious green, be-ribboned
Circling for some questions,
A coupla clear cases of bad complexion

Just unwholesome, twinned in Clearasil,
Marred by travel hardship.

And still divided, after time and talk,
We took them to the jungle, where
In a cool, green glade (the river running)
Their faces were as raw as ever
(Her eyes ran deep, her voice relaxed)
La Tapachulteca waded naked.

You could not figure; all descended to the tomb.
A movie mogul admired her vestments—
Asked her to present her colors and
She did, all colors, reds, greens and yellows
The plumage of our favorite mythic birds.

And walking back, we talked like drunken
Iconographers, inspired old loons, two-by-two,
Fools. Then parting, loves, we are
Where nothing vale nada.

Dog Lake Satori

Yosemite 7/13/12

We are fickle when
With Sages, Maharishis, Beats
We unpack our memories
Balancing
So, after hiking up the wilderness trail
Assailed by unseen bears
Among smooth boulders and the leaning trees
Alpine-perfect Dog Lake provoked real tears
For all the bloody stupid things this man does
Wounding daughters and sons
Giving offense
To wives, girlfriends, friends
Though Yeats has educated me
With what his gallant Irish airman
Brought to mind, balanced, weighed
Considering a likely combat fate
I realize that
I have no mortal fight
Nor sudden death to face
But days of ordinary hours to spend
And somehow, to be decent.

Casablanca

NYC 7/13/72

I pull the hat down over my nose
And tilt forward, into this,
Playing it again. Wasn't this the place
Where I became a man?
Maybe not, but some other smoky city
Nearby. The time sure passes fast.

Humphrey swills his liquor
Trying to forget her, just as she walks in
through the door. One of those nights
I had a drink and lost myself on a street
Where all of the buildings were white.
Thank God it wasn't the Medina at Fez,
What a sinister twist! Seeing her face
At every turn, I'd never have gotten out.

Now I tip the hat back off my brow,
My Ricard isn't nearly as bitter,
While I'm still making the same
old mistakes. Christ! It was Fez
Where I turned twenty-one,
All alone, and no piano for miles.

"Empty-headed Man[1]" Begins to Tank in Early Round

Isla Holbox, Mexico
January 15, 2011

Empty lounges on the sand
Sunlit islands empty
Project Shangri-La on hold
Downtown and in the country

At resorts facing scant demand
Ghostly hotel structures stand and hold
Their posts in after neutron-bombing scenes
Dick and Jane-less

What happened to the fun-mad crowd,
Their Hawaiian shirts and flunkies;
Throwing money out the window
Like some junkie?

Most do their own wash
At home now, while
Empty Laundromats hang around
Signifying something

In short, whether Puritans or clowns
Have picked a palette for the vacant clouds,
They now buy black and white
While fresh ideas are down

[1] Empty-headed man, the species formerly referred to as homo sapiens

(Just give me) A Place to Stand

On the news they kept talkin' about
all of those foreign peoples
but there was nothin' about my brotha
so it got me thinkin'--what about us...
what about the boyz in the hood ?
–Ice Cube

I saw you yesterday on the corner
not knowing which way to turn
your hand up above your ear
scratchin' a wooly head
questioning a foggy brain

from here it looked like
the sidewalk might teeter
and you would leave your feet
tossed off at a crazy angle
coat dangling back

this is the way the world turns
nowadays, nothing sacred
nothing ventured
in the fields of the absolute
nothing gained

only the boys of dissolution
hanging onto their codes of honor
won't let a name be taken in vain
their likely answer's a blast from the past
running against our tolerant grain

Between Me, The Sea and My Old Man

For my father

Here I sit
Between South Florida's
Hell bent civilization
And out by the Pompano Light
The deepest blue
Wondrous sea
All that we need
Clean creation of the
Clear compassionate mind
When we hit it right
Any tree in the garden
Good picture to see
Crayola kite surfers gone now
From the inked night
They tossed fantastic before
Now, the Pompano Light winks
I think of something to do or
Say for my dying Old Dad
Some dedication
Something for the difference
Like I told him on his hospice bed
Look: the sky out over the Everglades
Looks blue like it does
Hung for the Caribbean
The clouds stack up
Much the same as they do
Over Cozumel or Negril
When I asked him if this
Resembled Pago Pago

He said the Japs there
Fell right out of the trees
I mean you could cross
Some kind of ocean
To find meaning
Around a dying man
To find a last word
From a dutiful son
Share a laugh
Who remembers wherefore?
Dad, he wasn't a devil much
Sailed the war-torn & nautical sea
Made me
Step out into this predicament
Just about everyone bent
Said his piece:
Easy does it.
Thanks

Evidently An Angel

For Ethel Raiford

Skeptical, I still want proof
Of the existence of God
Honestly, I never
Needed it much
Although I realized lately
That I have known an angel

No searing vision --
For sixteen years Ethel lived
Across Allegheny Ave from us
She'd walk to the store for groceries
And tend her garden constantly
Until she died last month, at 91

We never heard an unkind word
Although she might laugh
At my Devilish remarks
She never complained—
After her soldier husband passed in Germany
Ethel came home with her children
Raising them alongside two nieces, bereft of parents

Oliver and I attended her funeral service
Down by Georgia Avenue recently
Funny, the two ladies we bought our house from
Came in from Philly
Evidently, Ethel made an impression
So did her granddaughter, 6'6" atop

Spiked heels. She plays in Europe now
We're hoping for a WNBA career

What is poetry? Who cares?
Ethel, evidently an angel, inhabits
These words, for this skeptical man
Who wonders if you get religion
Attending a funeral service
Down by Georgia Ave
(Pushing 92, Ethel never did accept
Any ride to fetch groceries)

That service where
For the finale
We watched a video of Aretha
Live at the piano
Singing *Amazing Grace*
That saved a wretch like me?

Hear That Tranquil Sitar Music?

I.

Destroyers and re-builders are gay
Irish Poet Yeats somewhat said
(Read joyous for gay
This day of the politically correct)
Now warmongering cynics knock
Down Mideast targets and re-erect
Their awful power to project
And rank-and-file Humanity
With all that fine phrase means
May with taxes and real sweat
Pay the overdraft
Squeezed by stubborn Masters
To the very last

II.

You seek a little physic
For the view
Do something
What would you do?
You looked in at Auschwitz
Just a little late
Preparing a bed for Gaza boys
The comfy homeless grate
What's to be done?
The question remains
Pick a good day to die like Cochise
Sulk in the tent with Achilles
Hang with Hamlet, rack your brains

III.

Population has exploded
And land's dear
But as soon as there were
Two Cro-Magnons
There was one fear
He'll get it, I won't
I'm doing this
No you don't!
My girl's hot
While yours is just squat
Consider the vast superiority
Of my Robot
He runs forever, we rot

IV.

Aristotle never swooned
But it doesn't matter
Your recent appeal to rationality
Returned without comment
From the Mad Hatter
Still, there's beauty in the world today
Poets, priests and philosophers
Remind us to be joyous (or otherwise, gay)
Let all music boxes sound dulcet tones
Feel that tingling feeling in your bones
The riddle of Life's solved: we'll outlaw Unions,
And hire our high-tech brothers—a chicken in every pot
In every Barcalounger, our Pain and Suffering Clones.

Night of Bruises

ALAN BRITT

All Ye Need To Know

Startled like Maine Coon in a room
full of strangers late one afternoon,

I remember the ticket coachman,
but I don't remember you.

I remember a feline soul, such as it
was, but I don't remember you.

So, I close my eyes & dream
of oilcloth sails meant for you,

& sail we do on abalone wings
throughout adolescent bougainvillea

& musky misfortunes releasing a
poetic virus that the universe wedges

between us, which is neither here
nor there, but for better & for

worse, I built a boat called love that
floats, & that is all ye need to know.

Crossing the Walt Whitman Bridge

They have named a bridge after Walt.

A massive extension of steel
& persistent weight.

This bridge connects daily lives
& supports the multitudes
nonstop 24 hours a day.

Walt would surely be proud.

But the true bridge,
the one he created
from our lives to the infinite,
is the one I'm crossing now
between the shores of my solitude.

The Secretaries

1.

Leaning from Brooklyn skyscrapers
secretaries
type hieroglyphs
across the clouds.

The blue afternoon.

The afternoon greets them
as equal lovers.

Stenographers emerge from mariposa hibernation.

Lovers in silk Armani suits.

A mythic Uncle with a damaged
liver
stumbles into Mass
at dawn.

His pockets inside out.

The bandoneon
tracing Donne's compass tip
rocks a cradle
woven from straw.

2.

Certain women,
especially those
predisposed
to common amnesia,
resemble the yellow lightning
staining elephant ear plants,
waists attached
to gravity
as their roots roam the darkness.

Tenderness oozes
between the secretaries' exposed hips.

I fall backwards
into a net
of drunken bats
gathered at an after-hours tavern.

My insufferable lover
arrives
with a knife
in her heart.

Crumbling to my knees
I kiss
her suffering hands.

The bandoneon
swirls
the tavern's darkness
around us.

Stars flicker
then vanish
into ashes.

The Tavern of Lost Souls

About the color of amber
asleep in a drawer
at a North Dakota fossil lab
an ant descends the crack
of a sidewalk
just below
my approaching Reebok.

I carry the shadow
of Nagasaki
in my walk.

However, my true agenda
is not cruelty.

As a matter of fact,
each morning around 12 PM
the mayor of my village
walks his burro
past the Chamber of Commerce.

Women make important decisions
while our men drive SUV's
to the local reservoir
in search of the Wild Man.

(Fewer capital crimes
are committed this way.)

Adolescents, mute since birth,
stitch fantasy tattoos
across each other's shoulders and lower backs
with the lethal precision of Andre Breton
and Tristan Tzara.

Extended families mingle
the local watering hole.

They cross their shriveled legs
while lighting up a stick
and growl into muddy drinks
all various shades of amber
asleep in drawers
at a fossil lab
somewhere near North Dakota.

Finally, just around midnight,
a shabby guitarist, with crescent
moon scar on his forehead
and a busted hip, saunters
into the tavern of lost souls.

Glorious Thursday

Fireflies tattoo twilight's torso
that resembles Nijinsky's tights.

On cable TV two dry-cleaned
bodies embrace.

One maple syrup rabbit
screeches rusty warning
to his mate in harm's way;
I whisper that we're here—
my Bichon & me—
before mate vaporizes
below thick forsythia.

Croakers plunder darkness.

AC fans & Yokohama tires
like maestro flicks of the wrist
lick the asphalt.

.38 caliber raindrops shatter
the asbestos roof & invite
eggplant's juvenile blossoms
with goldenrod stamens
to a romantic evening
at a candlelit hideaway.

Croakers give way to creepers,
creepers to cicadas, & like poets
not fully indoctrinated, cicadas

become cheetahs, cheetahs
exhausted by DNA yet intently
focused upon their next meal.

Childhood Confessions

I was adopted at six weeks.

I was ecstatic!

While young I pulled some pranks . . . nothing
too serious.

I paraded Mom's cashmere sweater
across the hardwood floor;
she wasn't pleased.

I rummaged Dad's closet & absconded
a deerskin slipper—
admonished for that.

I once grabbed a chocolate chip cookie bag
spilling garbage from a stainless steel can
across the kitchen tiles.

I heard about that for weeks.

But I matured, learned right from wrong
& respected household rules, learned
to play well with others, stopped
teasing the cat & even grew fond
of my Maine Coon sister.

I often wished Dad had more time to teach
me some games—I had energy to spare.

I sometimes begged Mom to close her laptop
& go for strolls around our neighborhood.

She was busy; I could see that.

But I amused myself; I made do.

I grew fast & avoided trouble, mostly.

Recently, Mom & Dad brought home a baby.
They named him Tom. He smells funny,
but I think I love him. A baby brother!
I circled the house exuding jubilation.

Then, suddenly, the surprise of my life.

One morning Dad walked me to the car & drove me
to a building with cinderblock walls & concrete floor.

I'll never forget; I'd just turned five & was overjoyed
for our expanding family.

Dad patted my head, closed the chain-link door,
& left me sitting on that concrete floor.

I've been here over a month. No sign of Mom,
no sign of Dad.

My name is Mason. I'm a pitbull/shepherd mix.

The terrier next to me was carried away this morning.
She was 14, at least, cataracts in both eyes.

The guy opposite, hound mix, spends all day shriveled
in a corner, tail coiled around his belly.

God, I'm lonely & confused. Mom, Dad, if you
can hear me, please come & get me.

Cesar Vallejo

Volcanic eyes

Aardvark gait

Soul a chrysalis & also
a papoose to tuck his family
into at night

Dreams swirled like
Van Gogh's *Starry Night*

His poems were fists
full of scorpions

Going Dorian

DAVID CHURCHILL

Bishop Asbury on Horseback

16th & Mount Pleasant Streets

It is June and the grass is high:
no one has mowed
this pasture yet—
Still the Bishop plods on,
oblivious to the sun;
where he is
it's been raining for days.

Old Revelator droops his head,
footsore and weary,
but the man on his back
is not tired: he rides
with one finger
tucked in his book,
a few crumbs of johnny-cake
all the sustenance he needs.

From the front you see
the past night in the cabin
at the foot of the tree-cliff,
where he knelt with the parents
whose child had been called
beyond the crest of a hill;

men have their feet
in the earth at all times
in this country;
in front of its mystery

they can only kneel
in order to get closer to it—
but there were too many
for the Bishop to stay long . . .

Only the old men
on the benches behind him,
easing their bones,
see the spires before him.

DAVID CHURCHILL

The Year I Didn't Go to School in Ankara, Turkey

Always the sky would be a dome
with the sun on the inside
as I walked down the hill,
taking a back road,
hearing the muezzin's call
broadcast over the valley,
and a donkey bray—

until my feet touched earth again.
Then the nests of storks
on their chimneys,
empty since autumn,
would be dusted with snow,
and workmen in waistcoats
shoveled cement
up the sides of slow buildings.

Behind me in the Twenty-Third of May
the house would be cold,
only Mom still asleep.
Soon Mehmet would arrive
to stoke the furnace,
shovel a little coal,
a man with two wives,
an old one in the country,
a new one in the city.

A hundred hours staring
at tea urns and tambourines—
eighty hours in doorways—

twenty hours on a bench
in Youth Park—
ten hours in a train-station—

an hour more waiting
for the sun to go down . . .

Memorial to Confederate Dead

Old Town, Alexandria

He stands,
contemplating something
at his feet:
the effects of winter
rain perhaps,
or sleet—
though on occasion
carnations appear,
as if his downturned eyes
had raised them
from genuine earth:

how the sun shone
on dew-stilled lupines—
the swish of feet
through wet timothy—
the spring-like call of a wren
across dawn meadows
before the first deaths—
the grief of bugles
still lives in present horns;

but more
than a lost morning,
more than echoed voices
that have lost
their source,
more than the metaphysics
of defeat:

gone the trumpeter,
gone the drum;
gone pennants
jumping in the breeze—
gone the cause.

DAVID CHURCHILL

Driving to Jimmy Cone's

Damascus, Maryland, 1992

All over the county
men who have never heard
of Tiepolo
drive under a sky
he perfectly foresaw,

and painted on a ceiling
in Europe somewhere,
three hundred years ago—
except for the putti.

Here putti
are in the back-seat,
visions of sundaes
melting on steeples
and cornfields.

Bug-zappers speak
to the dusk, and
as the crowd gathers
its light to itself,

a lampshade ignites
in the leaves of an oak.

Big Dog Walk

If you could speak
you would tell me
why this ground
is so exciting.

We passed it yesterday,
a hundred times before;
not worth a sniff—
There's nothing on it.

A late-spring fawn
born after its time,
in broad daylight:
him you don't sniff.

You give him a wide
berth.

Going Dorian

We came into cucumber
harvest
and sheepfold,
sacred
to the goddess,
place of barley
and horseraising
place,
the sons of Herakles,

and afterwards
took up the tactics
of the heavy equipment man,
marching all night
under ninety weight
of bronze; coming out
at dawn on a narrow plain,
stumbling
over broken ground,
unable to close ranks,
but Orthia was kind
and we spread into dove-cote
and as far away as gate.

But we loved ever
the geography of skin,
the scrape of a strigil
over bare limbs,

and the choristers,
singing:

his hair was hyacinths,
his lips like myrtle leaves,
his eyes were sunfilled
coves where boys dove
for octopus and conchs,
and his thighs
were the slopes of mountains
robed in ice and snow . . .

Those are his shinbones
woven in the wall,
that femur set beside them
was his friend.

On a Refusal to Convict a Low-Level Drug Dealer While the Sacklers Endow Another Museum

Jury Duty, Washington, DC 2018

He sits directly across from me,
Daquan—or something—
A bearded young man; give him
a boater and white skin

and he could be Amish.
The judge reads the charges.
I hear but don't hear.
I hear the rustle of a Grecian

breeze through silver trees,
watch shadows slant across stone.
We sit in the area
reserved for the chorus.

I'm sure a breeze sighs
through coal-town hollows too,
when coal-trains racket by,
where barbecue grills and old cars

rust from the inside out,
and American-flag curtains
grow stiff in trailer-park windows . . .
The cause of all sighs

sifts down from on high.
There petals of thornless roses
perfume white halls

where the bodies of gods
gather like clouds
on a day that does not rain.

In vain let the young man
come forth
for destruction—
In vain do we cry:
how can there be justice,
without a capital J?

Contributors

MARIANNE SZLYK

Marianne Szlyk is a professor of English and Reading at Montgomery College. She also edits *The Song Is...*, a blog-zine for poetry and prose inspired by music (especially jazz). Her first chapbook, *Listening to Electric Cambodia, Looking up at Trees of Heaven*, is available online at Kind of a Hurricane Press. Her second chapbook, *I Dream of Empathy*, is available on Amazon. Her poems have appeared in *The Ekphrastic Review, of/with, bird's thumb, Cactifur, Mad Swirl, Setu, Solidago, Red Bird Chapbook's Weekly Read*, and *Resurrection of a Sunflower,* an anthology of work responding to Vincent Van Gogh's art. Her full-length book, *On the Other Side of the Window*, is now available from Pski's Porch and Amazon. She invites you to stop by her blog-zine and perhaps even submit some poems: http://thesongis.blogspot.com

Acknowledgements:

"Astoria at Dawn" appeared in *Setu*. "Saturday Morning" was published in *Quill and Parchment*. "Abandoned" is part of Zoetic Press' anthology *Write Like You Are Alive 2016*. "The Summer After the Bridge Closed" appeared in *Duane's PoeTree*. "The Last Days of Fusion" and "Riding into Charles Street Station" were published by Eos: *The Creative Context*. "Facing East at Dawn," "Alternative History in Staunton, Virginia," and "Woolworth's, 1970" appeared in *Mad Swirl*. "Rainy Living" is from *Carcinogenic Poetry*. "The Social Work Assistant in Briarwood" appeared in *Wagon Magazine*. "Alternative History in Staunton, Virginia", "The Last Days of Fusion" and "Riding into Charles Street Station" appeared in *On the Other Side of the Window*. "York Beach, 2006" originally appeared in *Poppy Road Review*. "Thelma at HR-57" was published in *Mad Swirl*. "If My Mother is in Purgatory" was included in *Mermaid's Mirror*, an anthology by Madness Muse Press. "The Social Work Assistant in Briarwood" is forthcoming from *The Wagon Magazine*.

ETHAN GOFFMAN

Ethan Goffman is an environmental writer and national reporter for Mobility Lab. His poems have appeared in *Mad Swirl, Madness Muse*, and *Setu*. His journalism has been published in *EarthTalk*, *The Progressive*, *E: The Environmental Magazine*, *Grist*, and elsewhere. For six years, he authored the weekly *SSPP Blog*. Ethan is the author of *Imagining Each Other: Blacks and Jews in Contemporary American Literature* (State University of New York Press, 2000). He teaches at Montgomery College.

Acknowledgements:
"The Force Is Not with Me" and "Taxonomy of History" were originally published in *Mad Swirl.*

JAN STARKEY

Jan Starkey has a B.A. and an M.A. in English. She has taught English at the secondary school level and education courses at the college graduate school level. She has received several fellowships for poetry as well as fiction. Jan has studied poetry with Peter Klappert and Bruce Snider, and fiction with Kathryn Davis and Jay McInerney. She also likes to paint, take photographs, and create collages.

JOHN MACDONALD

John MacDonald is a Maryland poet. His work has appeared in numerous publications, including *Gargoyle Magazine*, *The Doctor T. J. Eckleburg Review*, *Poetry Quarterly*, *Dual Coast Magazine*, and *50 Haikus*. In 2013, a selection of his satirical, narrative poems were adapted for stage performance, as part of the Performetry series at BloomBars in Washington, DC, sponsored by Sanctuary Theatre, Inc., Poets & Writers, and the DC Commission on the Arts & Humanities. He has also been guest poet for the DC improvisational comedy troupes Poetic License and Poetic Justice.

ALAN BRITT

Alan Britt has published over 3,000 poems nationally and internationally in such places as *Agni, The Bitter Oleander, Bloomsbury Review, Borderlands: Texas Poetry Review, Christian Science Monitor, Confrontation, English Journal, Epoch, Flint Hills Review, Gallerie International* (India), *Kansas Quarterly, Letras* (Chile), *Magyar Naplo* (Hungary), *Minnesota Review, Missouri Review, New Letters, Northwest Review, Pedrada Zurda* (Ecuador), *Poet's Market, Queen's Quarterly* (Canada), *Revista/Review Interamericana* (Puerto Rico), *Revista Solar* (Mexico), *Roanoke Review, Steaua* (Romania), *Sunstone, Tulane Review*, and *The Writer's Journal*. His interview at The Library of Congress for *The Poet and the Poem* aired on Pacifica Radio, January 2013. He has published 16 books of poetry. He teaches English/Creative Writing at Towson University.

Acknowledgements:
"Crossing the Walt Whitman Bridge" (Traversând podul Walt Whitman) (English/Romanian) appeared in: Ars Longa Press, *Iasi*, ROMANIA: 2017, and *Alianza: 5 U.S. Poets in Ecuador*, CypressBooks, Rio Rico, AZ: 2015 and *Bodies of Lightning*, CypressBooks, Rio Rico, AZ: 1995; "The Secretaries" appeared in *The Hurricane Review* and *Resurrection of a Sunflower*, Catfish McDaris and Marc Pietrzykowski, curators, Pski's Porch Publications: 2017; "Tavern of Lost Souls" appeared in *Refined Savage Poetry Review* and *Resurrection of a Sunflower*, Catfish McDaris and Marc Pietrzykowski, curators, Pski's Porch Publications: 2017; "All Ye Need to Know" appeared in the *Zaira Journal* (Philippines): (Summer 2016); "Cesar Vallejo" in *First Literary Review East*, January 2017 and *Resurrection of a Sunflower*, Catfish McDaris and Marc Pietrzykowski, curators, Pski's Porch Publications, 2017 and "Glorious Thursday" appeared in *The Peregrine Muse* (2016).

ANNIE FINCH

Named "one of the central figueres in contemporary American poetry" by the *Dictionary of Literary Biography*, Annie Finch is the author or editor of more than twenty books. Her work has been traznslated into numerous languages and received such honors as the Robert Fitzgerald Award and the Sarasvati Award for Poetry. Best known for her poetry, Finch also writes literary and cultural essays, textbooks, and plays, and her work has been included in such anthologies as the *Penguin Book of the Sonnet*, the *Penguin Book of Twentieth-Century American Poetry*, and the *Norton Anthology of World Poetry*. Her notable books include *Among the Goddesses, The Body of Poetry, Calendars, Eve*, and *Spells: New and Selected Poems*. Finch wrote the memorial poem for the 9/11 attacks that accompany Meredith Bergmann's sculpture installed at the Cathedral of St. John the Divine in New York City as well as the keynote poem for the National Museum of Women in the Arts' Inauguration of the Women's Poetry Timeline.

Acknowledgements

"Spells" originally appeared in *Spells: New and Selected Poems* (Wesleyan University Press, 2013)

DAVID CHURCHILL

David Churchill is a poet and writer living in Washington DC. He is the author of a novel, three books of poetry and a play. His work is available on Amazon at: amazon.com/author/davidbchurchill

Acknowledgements

"Memorial to Confederate Dead" and "Driving to Jimmy Cone's" are from *Lucid Waking*; "Bishop Ashbury on Horseback" and "The Year I Didn't Go to School in Ankara, Turkey" from *Poetry is Mindfulness*; "Big Dog Walk" and "Going Dorian" from *The Going-Under of the Evening-Land*; "On a Refusal to Convict a Low-Level Drug Dealer While the Sacklers Endow Another Museum" will appear in the forth-coming *Homeless God Bless*.

REID BARON

Reid Baron lives with his wife Deborah Gay, a painter and para-educator in Takoma Park, Maryland. They have two grown sons, Alexander and Oliver. Reid edited and published *galleries magazine, a guide to Washington /Baltimore art spaces* for 35 years, retiring in 2017. He was also previously editor of *The Takoma Park Newsletter*, and *Contato*, Journal of the Brazil Network.

Reid worked as Portuguese-English translator and journalist during his residence in Brazil, 1973-1978. *Witches' Coffee*, an e-book novella set in Brazil, can be downloaded at Amazon. *Shoot the Breeze*, a basketball novel not entirely about basketball, has recently been completed. He's been writing poetry and fiction for fifty years. As a poet, he has an affinity with the New York School.

CPSIA information can be obtained
at www.ICGtesting.com
Printed in the USA
BVHW050107151022
649246BV00001B/82